# Sacramento County Wildflowers

Illustrations and Text by Chris Wassermann

*Chris Wasserman*

Photos by Jan Fetler

*Jan Fetler*

D1601496

# Table of Contents

# About the Authors

**Chris Wassermann** (back cover photo-right)

Wildflowers have been my interest for a long time.  During a vacation in the mountains, when I was six, I asked so many questions about the flowers I saw that my mother, in desperation, bought a wildflower guide.

I did not start painting seriously until I retired from nursing and moved to Rancho Murieta. On walks near my home I was impressed with the many varieties of plants growing in fields and along roads.  Since there was much development planned in our area, I wanted to hold on to some of this fragile beauty.  That's when I started to paint the wildflowers.  Pretty soon I wanted to know more about my subjects.  I attended lectures and took a class in Field Botany, where I learned to look up information in books and on line.

After meeting Jan in 2009, and many joyful hikes together along the Cosumnes River and Deer Creek Hills, our interest became more focused.  This guide is the result.

**Jan Fetler** (back cover photo-left)

I have loved all plants since childhood.  Upon acquiring a 'real' camera at 21, my first subjects were wildflowers.  Through the intervening years, plants and flowers have continued to be my passion and I became a Master Gardener in Sacramento County in 2011.

My love of wildflowers re-emerged in 2009 when I met Chris.  We have spent many happy hours romping through the wildflowers we love, and I have learned so much from Chris.

Photos in this book were taken using digital cameras, recently a Nikon D90 SLR.  But I like to tell all would-be photographers, it's not the camera but the eye that formats the picture.  For more of my photos, visit my web site at www.plumjam.com.

# Introduction

The collection of photos and paintings for this book began when we met at a wildflower tour at a local garden club in 2009. I was leading the tour and Jan was the designated photographer for the day. We became friends and shared our love of roaming hills, meadows and woodlands in search of wildflowers. The idea for a wildflower field guide to help others enjoy this natural beauty grew like a seed planted in fertile soil.

Although Jan enjoys getting up close and personal with her flower subjects, we agreed photographs would be best used to show you what the plant looks like in a natural setting. My paintings give you the fine points of flowers, leaves and other details you can use to identify the plant you find.

This book includes the most common and easily noticed wildflowers in the Sacramento area. These plants also grow elsewhere in California and other parts of the West. We chose to omit thistles, of which there are many. Other plants were omitted because of lack of photo or painting. Every time we go out we find more flowers. We have to stop somewhere. There is always a second edition!

For purposes of this book we have organized plants by color: white, yellow and orange, pink, red and purple, and finally blue. Color is often in the eye of the beholder. When in doubt check a closely related color category. Also, the color sections are arranged with the palest first and next by bloom time. For example if the color of yellow is similar from plant to plant, the earliest bloomers will be first.

Plant names especially common names abound for some wildflowers. We have included as many as we could for each plant. Some are quite creative. Each plant also includes the botanical name along with information about habitat, size and features. The term (Introduced) means the plant is native to another part of the world.

We hope you enjoy this guide as much as we enjoyed creating it.

Chris Wassermann

# Flower Parts

Below are illustrations of terms used throughout the text in this book.

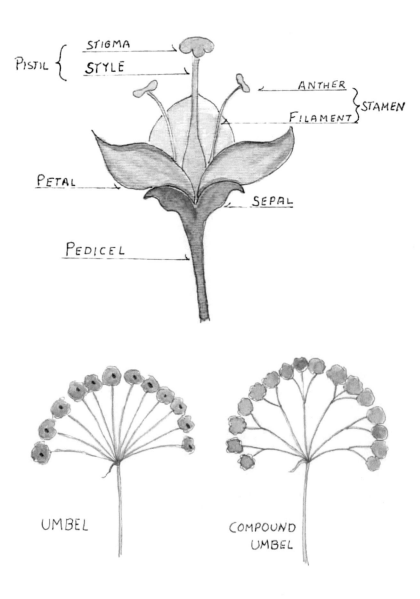

# White Flowers

White or whitish. Sometimes greenish, brownish or very pale pink, based on the viewer's first impression when finding the plant.

**Note**: The first 2 plants in this section have white flowers and also other colors. They are here to avoid repeating.

*Raphanus sativus*

**Wild Radish**

**Family:** Brassicaceae (Mustard)

**Plant size:** 1 to 5 feet

**Bloom time:** January to April

**Habitat:** Disturbed areas, roadsides

Flowers have dark purplish veins in the petals and are usually white or pink, but can be pale yellow or orange. Often grow with Mustards.

*Raphanus* means rapidly appearing, *sativus*: cultivated. Greens can be cooked like mustard greens. (Introduced)

## *Verbascum blattaria*

## Moth Mullein

**Family:** Scrophulariaceae (Snapdragon)

**Plant size:** 1 to 4 feet

**Bloom time:** May to October

**Habitat:** Disturbed places, roadsides

The flat flowers are white or yellow (inset photo) on tall spikes. The leaves and stems are not hairy. (Introduced)

9

*Daucus carota*

**Queen Anne's Lace, Bishop's Lace, Bird Nest**

**Family:** Apiaceae (Carrot)

**Plant size:** 1 to 3 feet

**Bloom time:** All year

**Habitat:** Roadsides, disturbed places

White flowers grow in flat umbel. When aging, they curl inward resembling a bird's nest. The middle of the flower head often has a pink to dark purple flower. The leaves are finely divided with a strong carrot like odor. The roots are edible when very young. Flowers keep well in bouquets. When growing near tomatoes, they will boost production.

## *Marah fabaceus*
## California Man Root

**Family:** Cucurbitaceae (Cucumber)

**Plant size:** 6 to 10 feet, vine

**Bloom time:** February to March

**Habitat:** Shrubby places, streambeds

Large, maple like leaves. Male flowers are pretty white stars, female flowers are much smaller white stars on top of round melon-to-be (ovary). Melons are round and spiny. The large root can be used to make lather similar to soap.

**Similar plant:** Taw Man Root, *Marah watsonii*. smaller leaves, more fig leaf like, melon has few spines.

11

*Lepidium nitidum*

**Shining Peppergrass**

**Family:** Brassicaceae (Mustard)

**Plant size:** 2 to 15 inches

**Bloom time:** February to May

**Habitat:** Disturbed areas, roadsides

The white flowers are tiny. What you most likely notice are the shiny reddish seedpods. This plant often grows in clumps.

## *Triteleia hyacinthina*

## White Brodiea, White Hyacinth, Fool's Onion

**Family:** Liliaceae (Lily)

**Plant size:** 6 inches to 2 feet

**Bloom time:** March to August

**Habitat:** Wet meadows

This sweet smelling, white flower has petal midribs that are green. The anthers are yellow or lilac.

The absence of an onion odor tells you that this is a *Triteleia* and not an *Allium*.

*Plagiobothrys nothofulvus*

**Popcorn Flower**

**Family:** Boraginaceae (Borage)

**Plant size:** 8 to 12 inches

**Bloom time:** March to May

**Habitat:** Grasslands, fields

White forget-me-not flowers coiled on slender hairy stems. Can create white hillsides. The entire plant can make purple stains when picked or bruised.

**Similar plant:** A miniature version, Vernal Pool Popcorn Flower (*Plagiobothrys stipitatus var. micranthus)* grows in vernal pools.

*Layia fremontii*

**Tidy Tips**

**Family:** Asteraceae (Sunflower)

**Plant size:** 6 to 10 inches

**Bloom time:** March to April

**Habitat:** Meadows, moist grasslands

The pale yellow carpets on spring slopes are Tidy Tips, the deep yellow ones are Goldfields. White tipped, yellow centered ray flowers surround yellow disk flowers with dark dots (anthers). The ray flowers are each cut into 3 lobes.

15

## *Limnanthes alba*

## White Meadow Foam

**Family:** Limnanthaceae (Meadow Foam)

**Plant size:** 4 to 12 inches

**Bloom time:** April to June

**Habitat:** Wet meadows, vernal pools

These flowers make depressions in wet meadows look like they are filled with foam. Bowl shaped white blossoms grow on slender stems. The petal veins are greenish, the leaves are linear.

Meadow Foam seed oil is a very high quality oil, similar to Sperm Whale oil. It is cultivated.

## *Aesculus californica*

## California Buckeye, California Horse Chestnut

**Family:** Hippocastanaceae
(Horse Chestnut)

**Size of plant:** To 40 feet, tree

**Bloom time:** April to May

**Habitat:** Canyons, dry slopes

Early spring leaves are followed by huge spires of white flowers. Leaves drop in mid-summer (Estivation) making the large seeds more notable in late summer and fall. The plant contains a glycoside (aesculine), which makes the flowers poisonous to honeybees. The Indians used crushed nuts to stun fish.

*Rubus ursinus*

## California Blackberry

**Family:** Rosaceae (Rose)

**Plant size:** 3 to 6 feet

**Bloom time:** April to May

**Habitat:** Moist, shaded fields, stream sides, roadsides.

California native. The leaves have green undersides, the flowers are white with rather narrow petals, the plant has many short thorny prickles.

*Convolvulus arvensis*

**Field Bindweed**

**Family:** Convolvulaceae
(Morning Glory)

**Plant size:** 1 to 5 feet, vine

**Bloom time:** April to October

**Habitat:** Disturbed places, fields

Arrowhead leaf shape with sharp
pointed lobes. One-half to 1-inch
flowers are white or tinged with
pink.

Stubborn common weed that is
very pretty. (Introduced)

## *Lithophragma bolanderi*
## Smooth Woodland Star

Photo © 2011 Jean Pawek. Used with permission.

**Family:** Saxifragaceae (Saxifrage)

**Plant size:** 8 inches to2 feet

**Bloom time:** May to June

**Habitat:** Open grassy slopes

White star flowers seem to float above the grasses. The petals are smooth.

**Similar plant:** *Lithophragma affine*, San Francisco Woodland Star has deeply lobed petals.

20

*Anaphalis margaritacea*

## Western Pearly Everlasting

**Family:** Asteraceae (Sunflower)

**Size of plant:** 6 inches to 3 feet

**Bloom time:** June to September

**Habitat:** Dry grassy fields, open woodlands (fuller and taller in moister areas)

White, papery flowers with yellow centers (actually the yellow centers are the flowers). They dry well and are used in dried flower arrangements. Strappy leaves are velvety. Brittle stems.

# *Achyrachaena mollis*

## Blow Wives

**Family:**  Asteraceae (Sunflower)

**Size of plant:**  4 to 15 inches

**Bloom time:**  April to May

**Habitat:**  Grasslands, woodlands

Orange, yellow flowers are easily overlooked. Mostly noticed for their seed heads, a large ball of silky white scales which look somewhat like flower petals.

## *Claytonia perfoliata*
## Miner's Lettuce, Winter Purslane

**Family:** Portulacaceae (Purslane)

**Plant size:** 4 to 12 inches

**Bloom time:** January to June

**Habitat:** Shady, moist places

Basal leaves are oval or spade shaped. Later pale pink or white flowers arise on top of a pair of fleshy round leaves that appear as one. Were used as food by both Indians and Pioneers. Now the plant is sometimes cultivated as a salad green.

23

## *Triteleia lilacina*

## Glass Lily

**Family:** Liliaceae (Lily)

**Plant size:** 4 to 20 inches

**Bloom time:** April to May

**Habitat:** Grassy meadows

Similar to White Hyacinth, *Triteleia hyacinthina*, but inner petals are shiny with what looks like tiny glass beads. The petal tips folding to point. The petal midribs are pink or brown, the anthers are blue. Sweet smelling flowers have no onion odor.

**Similar plant:** Glass Onion, *Allium hyalinum* is a larger plant with white flowers with a strong onion odor, likes moist conditions.

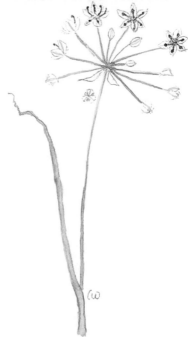

*Saponaria officinalis*

**Soapwort, Bouncing Bet**

**Family:** Caryophyllaceae (Pink)

**Plant size:** 1 to 4 feet

**Bloom time:** June to September

**Habitat:** Moist places, stream sides

Sweet scented white to pink flowers. 1 ½ to 3 inch leaves are opposite. The plant contains saponins, which are poisonous but have medicinal uses. (Introduced)

25

*Croton setigerus* (formerly *Eremocarpus setigerus)*

## Turkey Mullein, Dove Weed

**Family:** Euphorbiaceae (Spurge)

**Plant size:** 1 to 8 inches

**Bloom time:** June to October

**Habitat:** Woodlands, dry open spaces, disturbed places

Rosette of gray-green velvety leaves. Stems with tiny greenish flowers without petals. Older leaves often have pink edges. Birds love the seeds, but the plant is toxic to livestock. Indians used the plant to stun fish. Sometimes used ornamentally in rock gardens.

# Yellow and Orange Flowers

From pale to vivid yellow and finally dark yellow and orange.

*Phacelia cicutaria*

## Caterpillar Phacelia

**Family:** Hydrophyllaceae (Waterleaf)

**Plant size:** 1 to 3 feet

**Bloom time:** March to May

**Habitat:** Woodlands, rocky slopes

Pale yellowish or pale lavender dirty looking flowers on rangy stems. Oblong leaves with deeply lobed, toothed margins, almost ferny. Very fuzzy plant. Flower buds are in a hairy coil, resembling caterpillars.

*Dodecatheon clevelandii  ssp. patulum*

**Low Land Shooting Star, Padre's Shooting Star**

**Family:**  Primulaceae (Primrose)

**Plant size:**  3 to 10 inches

**Bloom time:**  January to February

**Habitat:**  Wet meadows

This tiny flower is yellow to creamy white, not pink like most Shooting Stars.  An early bloomer, it is easily overlooked.  It occurs only in California.  Found often on serpentine soils.

## *Lomatium utriculatum*

## Foothill Lomatium

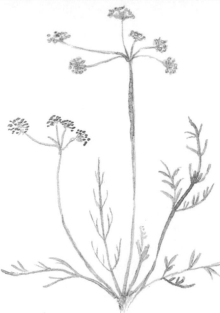

**Family:** Apiaceae (Carrot)

**Plant size:** 6 inches to 1 foot

**Bloom time:** February to May

**Habitat:** Moist grasslands, woodlands

Pale yellow flowers bloom very early. Leaves look ferny. Later blooming plants are taller.

*Castilleja campestris* (formerly *Orthocarpus campestris)*

**Field Owlsclover, Vernal Pool Field Owlsclover**

**Family:** Scrophulariaceae (Snapdragon)

**Plant size:** 4 to 6 inches

**Bloom time:** April to July

**Habitat:** Moist grassy fields, wetlands

Flowers are light to bright yellow, leaves and bracts are green. Unlike other *Castilleja*, they are not green root parasites (plants that produce some of their own nutrients, but use food from the roots of other plants).

Similar to Butter and Eggs, *Triphysaria eriantha*, but somewhat larger, and without red tinges.

31

### *Triphysaria eriantha (*formerly *Orthocarpus erianthus)*
### Butter and Eggs, Johnny Tuck

**Family:** Scrophulariaceae
(Snapdragon)

**Plant size:** 2 to 14 inches

**Bloom time:** March to May

**Habitat:** Grasslands

Three yellow sacks over a white
corolla (flower) tube with a red-purple
hooked beak. Upper leaves are also
reddish purple. In great masses they
give the meadows a yellow color with
reddish undertones.

*Triphysaria* are green root parasites,
having some green leaves for
photosynthesis, but also parasitize the
roots of other plants for ready-made
food.

*Cotula coronopifolia*

**Brass Buttons**

**Family:** Asteraceae (Sunflower)

**Plant size:** 8 to 16 inches

**Bloom time:** All year

**Habitat:** Vernal pools, muddy banks, marshes

Flat, yellow button like flower heads, like a daisy without petals. Can tolerate brackish water. (Introduced)

33

*Eschscholzia lobbii*

**Frying Pan Poppy, Lobb's Poppy**

**Family:** Papaveraceae (Poppy)

**Plant size:** 6 inches to 1 foot

**Bloom time:** February to March

**Habitat:** Open grassy fields

First of the poppies to bloom. Smaller and earlier blooming than California Poppy. The flat flower is bright yellow, not orange, petals are small and pointed. They close up on cloudy days.

## *Ranunculus californicus*
## California Buttercup

**Family:** Ranunculaceae (Buttercup)

**Plant size:** 6 inches to 2 feet

**Bloom time:** February to March

**Habitat:** Moist meadows, open grasslands, woodlands

Flowers are bright yellow with shiny petals. It has more petals (10 to 20) than Sacramento Buttercup (*ranunculus canus*) and is not as hairy. Ranunculus means "little frog".

**Similar plant:** Western Buttercup, *Ranunculus occidentalis* has only 5 or 6 petals.

35

# *Ranunculus canus*

## Sacramento Valley Buttercup

**Family:** Ranunculaceae (Buttercup)

**Plant size:** 1 to 3 feet

**Bloom time:** February to March

**Habitat:** Open grasslands

One of many Buttercups. 5 to 10 bright yellow shiny petals per flower.

*Mimulus guttatus*

## Seep Monkey Flower, Spring Monkey Flower

**Family:** Scrophulariaceae (Snapdragon)

**Plant size:** 6 inches to 2 feet

**Bloom time:** March to July

**Habitat:** Stream sides, wet meadows, vernal pools

Bright yellow flowers, often in great masses making yellow carpets on wet meadows. May have red dots in throat. Round to oval fleshy leaves and stems are edible.

37

*Leontodon saxatilis (*formerly *Leontodon taraxacoides)*

**Hawkbit, False Dandelion**

**Family:** Asteraceae (Sunflower)

**Plant size:** 8 to 14 inches

**Bloom time:** March to July

**Habitat:** Grasslands, disturbed places, roadsides

One of several dandelion look-alikes, with yellow ray flowers. The petals have toothed margins, the leaves have deeper cut edges. (Introduced)

**Similar plants:** *Hypochaeris radicata,* Hairy Cat's Ear tends to have more wavy leaf margins and forked stems, *Agoseris heterophylla*, California Dandelion is native, with finer seed heads and is hairy. The leaves are more wavy than serrated. Cat's Ear stems are solid and forked. Dandelion stems are hollow. All have similar uses as an edible green. Differences are hard to tell.

*Sanicula crassicaulis*

## Pacific Snake Root, Gamble Weed

**Family:** Apiaceae (Carrot)

**Plant size:** 1 to 3 feet

**Bloom time:** March to June

**Habitat:** Woodlands

The leaves are fairly large, like Maple leaves, with spiny margins. The very small flowers are yellow in a round umbel.

39

*Viola douglasii*

## Douglas Violet, Golden Douglas Violet

**Family:** Violaceae (Violet)

**Plant size:** 2 to 6 inches

**Bloom time:** March to May

**Habitat:** Open grasslands at low elevations

Bright yellow flower with reddish brown markings in the center. The backs of the two top petals are also red-brown. The highly divided leaves look ferny. It prefers serpentine soils.

*Lasthenia californica (*formerly *Lasthenia chrysostoma)*

**Goldfields**

**Family:** Asteraceae (Sunflower)

**Plant size:** 4 to 12 inches

**Bloom time:** March to May

**Habitat:** Grassy fields

In spring, turn hillsides into bright yellow slopes. They have linear, narrow, light green opposite leaves. Both stems and leaves are slightly hairy.

41

## *Lasthenia fremontii*

## Fremont's Goldfields, Vernal Pool Goldfields

**Family:** Asteraceae (Sunflower)

**Plant size:** 4 to 6 inches

**Bloom time:** March to May

**Habitat:** Meadows, drying vernal pools

Similar to Goldfields, *Lasthenia californica*, but petals are more reflexed, pointing downward. Leaves may have 1 to 3 pair of linear lobes.

## *Limnanthes douglasii*

## Douglas' Meadow Foam

**Family:** Limnanthaceae (Meadow Foam)

**Plant size:** 4 to 12 inches

**Bloom time:** March to May

**Habitat:** Wet meadows

*Limnanthes douglasii* has white flowers with yellow centers (see inset photo).

Sub species *rosea* is similar to White Meadow Foam but notched petals have pink veins and flowers age to pink. The leaves are pinnately divided.

*Calochortus luteus*

**Gold Nuggets, Gold Cups, Yellow Mariposa Tulip**

**Family:** Liliaceae (Lily)

**Plant size:** 18 inches to 2 feet

**Bloom time:** April to June

**Habitat:** Open fields

Bright yellow flowers with red-brown spot in center of inner petals. Each plant sends up a stem with as many as seven flowers.

*Tuberaria guttata*

**Spotted Rock Rose**

**Family:** Cistaceae (Rock Rose)

**Plant size:** 6 to 10 inches

**Bloom time:** April to May

**Habitat:** Disturbed places, grasslands

Small, striking yellow flower with a deep maroon center. Very delicate, it drops its petals easily. (Introduced)

## *Brassica rapa* (formerly *Brassica campestris*)
## Field Mustard

**Family:** Brassicaceae (Mustard)

**Plant size:** 1 to 6 feet

**Bloom time:** January to April, some all year

**Habitat:** Disturbed areas, along roadsides, cover crop under fruit trees, in vineyards

Flower is deep yellow. Used as a field green like spinach. (Introduced)

**Similar plant:** Black Mustard, *Brassica nigra*. The difference is mainly in the seed capsules.

46

*Eriophyllum lanatum*

**Wooly Sunflower, Oregon Sunshine**

**Family:** Asteraceae
(Sunflower)

**Plant size:** 6 inches to 2 feet

**Bloom time:** May to August

**Habitat:** Dry open places

Numerous large yellow flower
heads on long stems. Long hairs
give a gray appearance to both
leaves and stems.

## *Hypericum perforatum*

## St John's Wort, Klamath Weed

**Family:** Hypericaceae (St. John's Wort)

**Plant size:** 1 to 3 feet

**Bloom time:** May to August

**Habitat:** Roadsides, open fields

Yellow flowers on wiry stems. Petal edges sometimes have black dots. Leaves have tiny "perforations". Used medicinally to treat depression. It is toxic to livestock. (Introduced)

## *Centromadia fitchii* (formerly *Hemizonia fitchii*)

## Fitch's Spike Weed, Fitch's Tarweed

**Family:** Asteraceae (Sunflower)

**Plant size:** 6 inches to 3 feet

**Bloom time:** May to November

**Habitat:** Grasslands and roadsides

Pretty, bright yellow daisy like flowers with black dots (anthers) on forbidding looking, spiky stems that are branched. Sticky to touch.

## *Euthamia occidentalis*

## Western Goldenrod

**Family:** Asteraceae (Sunflower)

**Plant Size:** 1 to 4 feet

**Bloom time:** May to October

**Habitat:** Grasslands, meadows, stream banks

Small yellow flowers are bunched on long, slender, pale green stems. Long, narrow leaves.

*Grindelia hirsutula*

**Gum Plant**

**Family:** Asteraceae (Sunflower)

**Plant size:** 6 inches to 2 feet

**Bloom time:** May to September

**Habitat:** Usually in wetlands, but also in dry ditches

Yellow, daisy like flower on stiff, red-purple to brown stems. Long, slender, slightly toothed leaves. Cup below flower has claw like appendices that curl under.

**Similar plant:** *Grindelia camporum*, Valley Gum Plant has stems that look white washed with a gummy white sap. The "claws" are straight down.

51

*Mentzelia laevicaulis*

**Giant Blazing Star**

**Family:** Loasaceae (Loasa)

**Plant size:** 1 to 5 feet

**Bloom time:** June to October

**Habitat:** Sandy, rocky areas, roadsides

Large yellow 4 to 6 inch flowers on rangy stems. The petals are narrow and pointy, sepals are long and narrow, looking like more petals. Many long stamens look like a shaving brush. Gray-green leaves fold over along rib. The plant has distinctive seedpods.

## *Verbascum thapsus*
### Wooly Mullein, Common Mullein, Miner's Toilet Paper

**Family:** Scrophulariaceae (Snapdragon)

**Plant size:** 2 to 6 feet

**Bloom time:** June to September

**Habitat:** Roadsides, disturbed places

Soft, pale green wooly leaves are densely spaced up the long stem. Terminal spike has many small, yellow flowers, often with dark centers. (Introduced)

53

# *Heterotheca grandiflora*

## Telegraph Plant

**Family:** Asteraceae (Sunflower)

**Plant size:** 1 to 7 feet

**Bloom time:** September to December

**Habitat:** Open places, disturbed areas, roadsides

Dense, yellow flower heads on top of a leafy stem that is stiffly erect. Hairy leaves with strong odor.

*Eschscholzia caespitosa*

**Tufted Poppy, Collarless Poppy**

**Family:** Papaveraceae (Poppy)

**Plant size:** 6 inches to 2 feet

**Bloom time:** March to May

**Habitat:** Grassy areas

Smaller than California Poppy, it does not have the red platform beneath the petals. The flowers are more yellow than bright orange. Like all Poppies, it will close up on cloudy days. Found often on serpentine soils.

*Lotus corniculatus*

**Birds Foot Lotus, Birds Foot Trefoil**

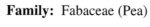

**Family:** Fabaceae (Pea)

**Plant size:** 6 inches to 2 feet

**Bloom time:** May to September

**Habitat:** Disturbed places, roadsides

Yellow to orange pea like flowers in a cluster at the end of the stem. Each leaf has 3 leaflets, but a pair of large leaf like stipules gives the appearance of 5 leaflets. Young plants are poisonous to humans, but not to livestock. (Introduced)

*Wyethia angustifolia*

**Narrow Leaved Mule Ears, California Compass Plant**

**Family:** Asteraceae (Sunflower)

**Plant size:** 6 inches to 2 feet

**Bloom time:** April to July

**Habitat:** Open grassy fields, slopes

The yellow, sunflower like blooms are on a hairy stem. The leaves are long and slender, also hairy.

*Helianthus annuus*

**Common Sunflower, Kansas Sunflower**

**Family:** Asteraceae (Sunflower)

**Plant size:** 1 to 10 feet

**Bloom time:** April to October

**Habitat:** Roadsides, open areas

The proverbial Sunflower. A very common, pretty weed with large heart shaped leaves. It is the state flower of Kansas.

*Holocarpha virgata*

**Sticky Tarweed, Yellow Flower Tarweed**

**Family:** Asteraceae
(Sunflower)

**Plant size:** 1 to 4 feet

**Bloom time:** August to
November

**Habitat:** Grasslands

Orange-yellow flowers start to
bloom from top of spike, later
flowers open down the stem.
Pinecone like branches on
entire plant. Sticky to the
touch with strong odor.
Sometimes young plants are
used as herbs.

# *Amsinckia intermedia*

## Common Fiddle Neck

**Family:** Boraginaceae (Borage)

**Size of plant:** 6 inches to 3 feet

**Bloom time:** March to June

**Habitat:** Oak woodland, grassland, disturbed places

Orange-yellow flowers in coiled spike like a shepherd's crook. When dried in hay is harmful to live stock. Lawrence's Goldfinches like the seeds.

Very common plant.

*Eschscholzia californica*

**California Poppy**

**Family:** Papaveraceae
(Poppy)

**Plant size:** 6 inches to 2 feet

**Bloom time:** March to October

**Habitat:** Open fields, meadows

The state flower of California.
Bright orange, they can turn a
hillside into gold. The 4 petals
form a large cup shaped bowl.
The leaves are lacy. Late season
flowers are smaller and paler,
even yellow. Reddish disk
platform under petals distinguish
this poppy from others. Flowers
close up on cloudy days.

*Anagallis arvensis*

**Scarlet Pimpernel**

**Family:** Primulaceae (Primrose)

**Size of plant:** 4 to 12 inches

**Bloom time:** March to September

**Habitat:** Disturbed places

Orange-red flowers with purple centers, in some localities flowers can be blue. Common garden weed (Introduced)

*Dudleya cymosa*

**Live Forever, Rock Lettuce, Canyon Dudleya**

**Family:** Crassulaceae (Stonecrop)

**Plant size:** 4 to 12 inches

**Bloom time:** April to July

**Habitat:** Rocky hillsides, rock outcroppings

Blue-green rosette of leaves gives rise to orange-red to yellow flower clusters on long stems.

*Mimulus aurantiacus* (formerly *Mimulus longiflorus*)

**Bush Monkey Flower, Sticky Monkey Flower**

**Family:** Scrophulariaceae (Snapdragon)

**Plant size:** 2 to 4 feet

**Bloom time:** April to June

**Habitat:** Dry slopes, woodlands

Yellow to orange flowers on long woody branches. Leaves and stems are sticky. Will grow on serpentine soil. The plant has some antiseptic properties and was used to speed healing of wounds.

# Pink Flowers

From pale to bright pink.

*Silene gallica*

**Common Catch Fly**

**Family:** Caryophyllaceae (Pink)

**Plant size:** 4 to 20 inches

**Bloom time:** February to July

**Habitat:** Disturbed places, roadsides, meadows

White to pinkish flowers with rounded petal tips. The calyx (below petals) has bristly purple ribs. The whole plant is quite hairy. (Introduced)

*Phyla nodiflora var. nodiflora*

**Lippia, Turkey Tangle, Frog Fruit**

**Family:** Verbenaceae (Vervain)

**Plant size:** 3 to 5 inches mat like

**Bloom time:** April to June

**Habitat:** Wet places, ditches, fields

White to pinkish flowers. Leaves are oblong, toothed. This plant is sometimes used as a lawn substitute or ground cover.

## *Keckiella breviflora*

## Bush Beard Tongue, Yawning Penstemon

**Family:** Scrophulariaceae (Snapdragon)

**Plant size:** 8 to 30 inches

**Bloom time:** May

**Habitat:** Rocky slopes, woodlands

Strange shaped pinkish white flowers open along slender willowy stems.

*Asclepias speciosa*

**Showy Milk Weed**

**Family:** Asclepiadaceae (Milk Weed)

**Size of plant:** 1 to 4 feet

**Bloom time:** May to August

**Habitat:** Woodlands, fields

Big flowers, pink or white, have curving hoods cupping inward. Large leaves velvety gray-green are oblong. The seeds have long, luxurious silky threads. Food for Monarch butterfly caterpillars. The Indians used the plant medicinally for stomach aches (the roots) and a tea for eye problems.

*Rubus discolor*

**Himalayan Blackberry**

**Family:** Rosaceae (Rose)

**Plant size:** 3 to 6 feet, vine

**Bloom time:** May to July

**Habitat:** Disturbed places, fields, roadsides

Leaves have white undersides, flowers are pink and larger than California Blackberries. They bloom and ripen later and have fewer but larger thorns. *Rubus* means bramble in Latin. (Introduced)

*Lotus purshianus*

**Spanish Lotus**

**Family:** Fabaceae (Pea)

**Plant size:** 6 inches to 3 feet

**Bloom time:** May to October

**Habitat:** Roadsides, grasslands, disturbed areas

Pretty little pale rose flowers on a gray-green plant that has long pale gray hairs.

# *Asclepias fascicularis*

## Narrow Leaf Milk Weed, Mexican Whorled Milk Weed

**Family:** Asclepiadaceae (Milk Weed)

**Size of plant:** 2 to 4 feet

**Bloom time:** June to September

**Habitat:** Dry fields, road banks

Pink tinged white small flowers in clusters. Linear leaves. Seedpods spill open to shed seeds with many silky hairs. The plant is food supply for Monarch butterflies.

*Erodium botrys*

**Long Beaked Filaree, Long Beaked Storks Bill, Scissors**

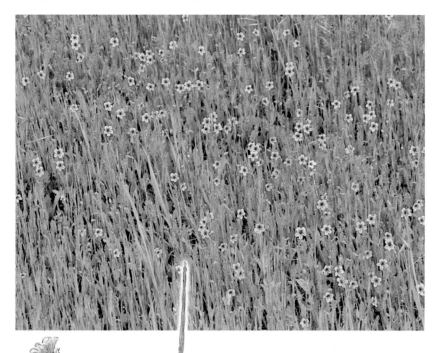

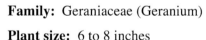

**Family:** Geraniaceae (Geranium)

**Plant size:** 6 to 8 inches

**Bloom time:** March to May

**Habitat:** Disturbed places, pastures, hillsides

Seed beaks are up to 5 inches long. Pretty pink cup like flowers can make carpets of magenta over a wasted area.

The seeds curl when dry, but straighten when wet, thus digging themselves into the ground with the first rains. (Introduced)

*Erodium cicutarium*

**Red Stem Storks Bill, Red Stem Filaree**

**Family:** Geraniaceae (Geranium)

**Plant size:** 6 to 8 inches

**Bloom time:** February to May

**Habitat:** Grasslands, disturbed places

Red stems in prostate rosettes. Small pink petals are separate from each other. Leaves are finely cut. Much smaller seedpods than Long Beaked Storks Bill. (Introduced)

**Similar plant:** White Stemmed Storks Bill, *Erodium moschatum*, the pinnate leaves have oval leaflets.

*Sidalcea hartwegii*

## Hartweg's Sidalcea, Checker Bloom

**Family:** Malvaceae (Mallow)

**Plant size:** 6 inches to2 feet

**Bloom time:** March to June

**Habitat:** Open fields, grassy slopes

A branched stem of several pink to purple flowers nod on long stems over grassy fields. Slender leaflets.

**Similar plants:** Lavender Vernal Pool Checker Bloom, *Sidalcea calycosa* grows on edges of vernal pools.

Alkali Checker Bloom, *Sidalcea hirsuta*, pink flowers on moist, grassy slopes.

## *Trifolium depauperatum*

## Cow's Udder Clover, Pale Sack Clover

**Family:** Fabaceae (Pea)

**Plant size:** 4 to 10 inches

**Bloom time:** March to June

**Habitat:** Fields, meadows, roadsides

Flowers are tiny inflated sacks in a cluster, looking like a cow's udder upside down. The 3 leaflets per leaf are narrow.

**Similar plant:** Bull Clover, *Trifolium fucatum*, has white spotted leaves and pale pink to white flowers in larger flower heads. Bloom somewhat later. There are close to 100 species of clovers found in California.

*Leptosiphon bicolor* (formerly *Linanthus bicolor)*

**Baby Stars**

**Family:** Polemoniaceae (Phlox)

**Plant size:** 1 to 4 inches

**Bloom time:** March to May

**Habitat:** Open fields, grassy slopes

These tiny bright pink flowers can create a pink hue over an entire field. The corolla (flower) tube is very long. Petals are at right angles with a yellow collar. Leaves look like tiny shaving brushes at intervals along the stem.

**Similar plant:** *Leptosiphon ciliatus*, Whisker Brush has dark rose spots on the petals and shorter corolla tubes.

*Dichelostemma volubile*

**Twining Snake Lily**

**Family:** Liliaceae (Lily)

**Plant size:** 2 to 5 feet

**Bloom time:** April to June

**Habitat:** Shrubby
undergrowth, shady hillsides

Pink, urn shaped flowers in an
umbel on a long pink twining
stem, that may be wrapped
around grasses or twigs (even
poison oak). Grow in rock
crevices and on steep slopes.

## *Trifolium hirtum*

## Rosy Clover, Rose Clover

**Family:** Fabaceae (Pea)

**Plant size:** 1 to 2 feet

**Bloom time:** April to June

**Habitat:** Disturbed sites, roadsides, fields

Common pink clover, turning roadsides pink. The whole plant is hairy. The fuzzy seed heads stay on till fall. (Introduced)

## *Trifolium resupinatum*

## Persian Clover, Reversed Clover

**Family:** Fabaceae (Pea)

**Plant size:** 6 to 12 inches

**Bloom time:** April to June

**Habitat:** Disturbed places

Small round pink flower on a creeping, prostrate plant. Sometimes used as ground cover. (Introduced)

*Geranium molle*

**Wooly Geranium, Dove's Foot Geranium, Soft Cranes Bill**

**Family:** Geraniaceae (Geranium)

**Plant size:** 3 to 8 inches

**Bloom time:** April to September

**Habitat:** Shady woodlands, disturbed areas, grasslands

Pretty, small, pink flowers with heart shaped petals. Leaves relatively round, small and hairy.

Geraniums have palmately lobed leaves. Fillaries (*Erodium*) have side lobed leaflets. (Introduced)

*Zeltnera venusta* (formerly *Centaurium venustum)*

**Charming Centaury, Canchalagua**

**Family:** Gentianaceae (Gentian)

**Plant size:** 4 to 15 inches

**Bloom time:** May to August

**Habitat:** Dry slopes, disturbed areas

Pretty, hot pink to magenta stars with white centers. Leaves are opposite and lance shaped. Many flowers per stem.

## *Clarkia unguiculata*

## Elegant Clarkia

**Family:** Onagraceae (Evening Primrose)

**Plant size:** 1 to 3 feet

**Bloom time:** May to June

**Habitat:** Grassy slopes, woodlands

Showy flowers with four pink outer petal lobes on a threadlike base. Petals may have a dark-red spot. Spindly, rangy plant with narrow leaves is widely branched.

83

*Petrorhagia dubia (*formerly *Tunica prolifera)*

**Hairy Pink, Wild Carnation**

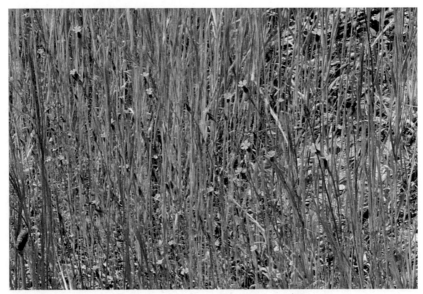

**Family:** Caryophyllaceae (Pink)

**Plant size:** 1 to 2 feet

**Bloom time:** May to June

**Habitat:** Woodlands, disturbed fields

Grassy stems topped by a small cluster of bright pink carnation like flowers. Each petal has deep pink markings and is somewhat heart shaped. Leaves are short and like a carnation's. (Introduced)

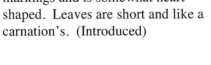

*Vicia villosa*

**Winter Vetch**

**Family:** Fabaceae (Pea)

**Plant size:** 2 to 5 feet

**Bloom time:** March to July

**Habitat:** Open fields, disturbed places

It has 10 or more violet to purple flowers on a raceme. Sometimes the flowers are white or pink. The pinnately compound leaves and stems are slightly hairy.

Common weed. (Introduced)

85

## *Lamium amplexicaule*

## Clasping Henbit

**Family:** Lamiaceae (Mint)

**Plant size:** 2 to 16 inches

**Bloom time:** February to May

**Habitat:** Disturbed places, roadsides

The flowers are tubular, hot pink to purple with pretty dark dots on the lower petals. The rounded upper leaves clasp the stem. (Introduced)

## *Calandrinia ciliata*

## Redmaids

**Family:** Portulacaceae (Purslane)

**Plant size:** 4 to 20 inches

**Bloom time:** February to May

**Habitat:** Dry open fields.

Shiny, hot pink flowers that open later in the day in sunny weather. Blooms only last a few hours, but masses of plants can make a field of red-pink in the bright spring sun. Two sepals under the flower cups are typical of the Purslane family.

The black seeds and leaves were used as food by the Indians.

*Vicia sativa*

**Spring Vetch**

**Family:** Fabaceae (Pea)

**Plant size:** 1 to 3 feet

**Bloom time:** March to July

**Habitat:** Fields, disturbed places

It has one or two large hot pink blossoms per leaf axil.

Common weed. (Introduced)

## *Mimulus tricolor*

## Vernal Pool Monkey Flower, Tricolor Monkey Flower

**Family:** Scrophulariaceae (Snapdragon)

**Plant size:** 2 to 4 inches

**Bloom time:** March to May

**Habitat:** Moist meadows, vernal pools

Pretty little purple flowers that have triangular burgundy spots and bright yellow "cheeks". The leaves are oval.

**Similar plant:** *Mimulus angustatus*, Purplelip Pansy Monkey Flower has a very long corolla (flower) tube, round burgundy spots, and linear leaves.z

# Red and Purple Flowers

Red flowers here tend to the brownish hue.  Purple tend toward the warmer side of the color family.  Also check the Blue Flowers section if the flower you see doesn't appear here.

*Aristolochia californica*

## Dutchman's Pipe

**Family:** Aristolochiaceae (Pipevine)

**Size of plant:** 8 to 10 feet, vine

**Bloom time:** February to March

**Habitat:** Along streams in woodlands

Brown-green flowers lined with purple or red in unusual tubular shape, like smoking pipes. Not carnivorous, but insects often get lost in the convoluted flowers.

Black Swallowtail butterflies often visit, since this plant is the only food source for their larvae. The caterpillars are black with red spots.

*Sanicula bipinnatifida*

## Shoe Buttons, Purple Sanicle

**Family:** Apiaceae (Carrot)

**Plant size:** 6 inches to 2 feet

**Bloom time:** March to May

**Habitat:** Meadows, fields, woodlands

Flowers are dark red to purple balls with feathery stamens on slender stems. In some areas the flowers can be yellow.

*Trifolium variegatum*

**White Tipped Clover**

**Family:** Fabaceae (Pea)

**Plant size:** 4 to 16 inches

**Bloom time:** April to June

**Habitat:** Open slopes, meadows

One of the prettiest clovers, it has burgundy red flowers with white tips. The leaflets are narrow, oblong with toothed margins. Strong, sweet smell.

**Similar plant:** Bearded Clover, *Trifolium barbigerum*, has dark red flowers with white upper half in a large green "punchbowl" bract. It grows in moist meadows and vernal pools.

*Trifolium willdenovii* (formerly *Trifolium tridentatum)*

## Tomcat Clover

**Family:** Fabaceae (Pea)

**Plant size:** 6 to 20 inches

**Bloom time:** April to July

**Habitat:** Damp grassy hills

Red-purple flowers in a wheel-like loose arrangement. The three leaflets are very narrow, serrated, and pointed.

*Symphyotrichum chilense* (formerly *Aster chilensis*)

**Pacific Aster, Chilean Aster**

**Family:** Asteraceae (Sunflower)

**Plant size:** 1 to 4 feet

**Bloom time:** July to November

**Habitat:** Dry open places, grasslands

Purple flowers with slender rays, strap like narrow leaves with broader leaves near base. This is a native plant, despite its name. Ironically, it does not occur in Chile.

*Collinsia heterophylla*

**Purple Chinese Houses, Innocence**

**Family:** Scrophulariaceae (Snapdragon)

**Plant size:** 6 inches to 2 feet

**Bloom time:** March to July

**Habitat:** Woodlands, shady places under oaks

Whorls of reddish purple flowers with white upper lips are reminiscent of pagodas. Flowers are often confused with Lupines, but the flower structure is different. The wing petals are connected to the keel petal like in a snapdragon.

97

*Dichelostemma multiflorum*

**Wild Hyacinth, Many Flower Brodiaea, Round Tooth Ookow**

**Family:** Liliaceae (Lily)

**Plant size:** 1 to 3 feet

**Bloom Time:** May

**Habitat:** Grasslands, hillsides

Lavender flowers in a dense rounded cluster 2 inches or more across atop a naked stem. There may be as many as 30 flowers on each stem. The individual flower is urn shaped rather than bell shaped.

## *Brodiaea elegans*

## Harvest Brodiaea, Purple Brodiaea

**Family:** Liliaceae (Lily)

**Plant size:** 14 to 16 inches

**Bloom time:** May to July

**Habitat:** Woodlands, grassy slopes, dry fields

Striking flowers in dry fields. Deep violet funnel-like flowers in a loose umbel, have 3 concave flat stamenoidia (sterile stamens) well away from the 3 long anthers.

**Similar plants:** Crown Brodiaea, *Brodiaea coronaria* flowers are more rosy, pinkish purple and stamenoidia are closely pressed to the anthers. Vernal Pool Brodiaea, *Brodiaea minor,* smaller pinkish purple, flower tube is constricted, blooms March to April, often only one or two flowers per stem. Purdy's Brodiaea, *Brodiaea purdyi,* a 3 to 12 inch plant, stamenoidia narrow spreading above petals, blooms April to June.

## *Verbena bonariensis*
## Purple Vervain, Brazilian Vervain

**Family:** Verbenaceae (Vervain)

**Plant size:** 3 to 6 feet

**Bloom time:** August to October

**Habitat:** Disturbed, wet places

Rough, hairy, coarse plant with small purple flowers and clasping leaves. There are many hybrid varieties for horticultural uses in gardens. (Introduced)

# Blue Flowers

From pale blue to sky blue to dark blue.  Some may appear to be purple in some light.

*Gilia tricolor*

**Birds Eye Gilia**

**Family:** Polemoniaceae (Phlox)

**Plant size:** 4 to 6 inches

**Bloom time:** March to April

**Habitat:** Woodlands, grassy slopes

Bowl-like violet, blue edged flowers with pale yellow to orange centers. There are tiny dark purple lines at the mouth of the flower tubes. Flowers form pale lavender carpets on grassy slopes.

On cloudy days they seem to disappear, since the blooms close up.

*Gilia capitata*

## Globe Gilia, Blue Headed Gilia

**Family:** Polemoniaceae (Phlox)

**Plant size:** 6 inches to 3 feet

**Bloom time:** April to June

**Habitat:** Grassy hillsides

Round balls of dark to pale blue flowers on tall stems. Stamen and style stick well out of the individual flowers.

## *Triteleia laxa*

## Ithuriel's Spear, Wally Baskets, Grass Nut

**Family:** Liliaceae (Lily)

**Plant size:** 1 to 4 feet

**Bloom time:** April to June

**Habitat:** Open grasslands, woodlands

Large blue flowers in an open umbel. The petals are flaring at a low angle, the mid veins are dark purple. They look like skinny Agapanthus. The long slender leaves are usually withered at bloom time.

## *Navarretia pubescens*

## Downy Navarretia, Downy Pincushion Plant

**Family:** Polemoniaceae (Phlox)

**Plant size:** 4 to 12 inches

**Bloom time:** May to June

**Habitat:** Woodlands, grasslands

Fuzzy little plant with a bouquet of bright blue-purple flowers on top. The leaves are finely divided and sticky.

**Similar plant:** *Navarretia leucocephala*, Needle or White Navarretia is smaller and has white flowers, found in vernal pools.

## *Veronica anagallis-aquatica*

## Water Speedwell, Water Brooklime

**Family:** Scrophulariaceae
(Snapdragon)

**Size of plant:** 6 inches to 2 feet

**Bloom time:** May to September

**Habitat:** Marshy places, creek
sides

Pale blue flowers, similar to
Forget-me-not. Large lance like
leaves attached directly to flower
stem. Edible. Flavor similar to
Watercress.

The Indians used the plant as an
expectorant tea.

*Trichostema lanceolatum*

**Vinegar Weed, Blue Curls, Camphor Weed**

**Family:** Lamiaceae (Mint)

**Plant size:** 4 inches to 2 feet

**Bloom time:** June to October

**Habitat:** Roadsides, dry fields, disturbed places

Strong smelling, hairy plant with purple-blue flowers. The flower is twisted so the long, curving stamens curl backwards to the stem. They were used to repel fleas, also as a cold and fever remedy.

The oils have phytotoxic (poisonous to other plants) properties.

107

# *Dichelostemma capitatum*

# Blue Dicks

**Family:** Liliaceae (Lily)

**Plant size:** 6 inches to 3 feet

**Bloom time:** January to May

**Habitat:** Grasslands, open woodlands

One of the first flowers to bloom. Purple-blue flowers in a dense umbel enclosed at the base by two metallic purple bracts. Stems are rather weak and bent. Leaves usually withered at bloom. After grass fires often very vigorous blooms next season.

Corms (bulbs) may be dormant for 10 years or more. Indians used the corms for food.

*Sisyrinchium bellum*

## California Blue Eyed Grass

**Family:** Iridaceae (Iris)

**Plant Size:** 4 to 20 inches

**Bloom time:** February to July

**Habitat:** Open grassy fields

Dark purple to blue, 6 petaled stars with bright yellow centers. Each stem has more than one flower.

**Similar plant:** Idaho Blue Eyed Grass, *Sisyrinchium idahoense* has pale blue flowers and only one flower per stem.

## *Downingia bicornuta*

## Horned Downingia

**Family:** Campanulaceae
(Bellflowers)

**Plant size:** 4 to 10 inches

**Bloom time:** March to June

**Habitat:** Moist meadows, vernal
pools

There are many varieties of
Downingia in this area. Blue and
lavender in color, they have small
differences in flower structure
between species. Some have dark
markings in the throat. All make
colorful carpets over mud as vernal
pools dry out in spring.

*Lupinus nanus*

**Sky Lupine, Douglas Lupine**

**Family:** Fabaceae (Pea)

**Plant size:** 6 inches to 2 feet

**Bloom time:** March to April

**Habitat:** Open grassland

Flowers are blue, aging to purple. The white area in the middle of the banner (top) petal that has black spots in it. The banner petal is wider than tall.

Valley lupine has flowers that are taller than wide and a hairy stem. They look slimmer.

## *Lupinus bicolor*

## Mini Lupine

**Family:** Fabaceae (Pea)

**Plant size:** 6 to 16 inches

**Bloom time:** March to June

**Habitat:** Hillsides, roadsides, open grasslands

Plant has slender, narrow leaflets. Flowers are much smaller than other lupines, having only 1 to 3 flower whorls.

They often grow with Sky Lupines, *Lupinus nanus*.

*Lupinus benthamii*

**Spider Lupine**

**Family:** Fabaceae (Pea)

**Plant size:** 1 to 4 feet

**Bloom time:** March to June

**Habitat:** Dry slopes

Deep-blue flowers with yellowish centers on tall slender stems. Leaves have very narrow linear leaflets, bringing spider legs to mind.

Stems and sepals are very hairy, making unopened buds look like they are wrapped in spider webs.

### *Lupinus microcarpus* (formerly *Lupinus subvexus*)

### Valley Lupine

**Family:** Fabaceae (Pea)

**Plant size:** 6 to 16 inches

**Bloom time:** April to June

**Habitat:** Hillsides, grassland, disturbed areas

Carpet hillsides with blue.

Similar to Douglas Lupine, *Lupinus nanus*, but more slender banner (top) petals and hairy stems.

## *Lupinus albifrons*

## Bush Lupine, Silver Bush Lupine

**Family:**  Fabaceae (Pea)

**Plant size:**  1 to 4 feet

**Bloom time:**  April to June

**Habitat:**  Foothill
woodlands, stream sides

Beautiful blue-violet flowers
on a woody plant.  It is the
only shrub-like lupine in the
Sacramento valley.

Since it is toxic to livestock,
it is often eradicated in
rangeland.

*Cichorium intybus*

**Chicory, Blue Saylors, Coffee Weed**

**Family:** Asteraceae (Sunflower)

**Plant size:** 1 to 4 feet

**Bloom time:** June to October

**Habitat:** Roadsides, disturbed places

Large, bright sky blue flowers on a woody, leafless stem. The basal leaves are similar to Dandelions. The roots can be roasted as a coffee substitute.

Plant is toxic to internal parasites, and is used as fodder for horses. (Introduced)

## *Delphinium variegatum*
## Royal Larkspur

**Family:** Ranunculaceae (Buttercup)

**Plant size:** 1 to 3 feet

**Bloom time:** March to May

**Habitat:** Grasslands, open woodlands

Very large, deep royal blue flowers. Leaf segments are folded and hairy.

**Similar plant:** *Delphinium hansenii*, Hansen's Delphinium, El Dorado Larkspur, has taller paler flowers in dense spikes, can even be white. Lower leaves are broad, barely divided. The plant blooms somewhat later.

# References

Hickman, James C. (Editor)
*Jepson Manual of Higher Plants of California*
Berkeley: University of California Press
3rd printing with corrections 1996

Fauver, Toni
*Wildflower Walks and Roads of the Sierra Gold Country*
Comstock Bonanza Press 1998

Niehaus Theodore F./Ripper, Charles L.
*A Field Guide to Pacific States Wildflowers*
"Peterson Field Guide"
Houghton Mifflin Co. 1976

Spellenberg, Richard
National Audubon Society
*Field Guide To North American Wildflowers*
Western Region
Alfred A Knopf, New York,
Thirteenth Printing 1994

Munz, Philip A.
*Introduction to California Spring Wildflowers of the Foothills, Valleys, and Coast*
University of California Press
Revised Edition 2004

Witham, Carol
*A Field Guide to the Vernal Pools of Mather Field*
California Native Plant Society 2006

Blackwell, Laird R.
*Wildflowers of the Sierra Nevada and the Central Valley*
Lone Pine Field Guide
Lone Pine Publishing 1999

Internet sources: Cal Flora, Cal photo, and others.

# Index

Made in the USA
Middletown, DE
14 November 2014